Borderline: Misunderstood

Willow Sykes

I would like to dedicate this book to my family, but especially to my mum who has been there for me through everything. She is my best friend, my teacher, and my inspiration. If it wasn't for her helping hand I wouldn't be the woman I am today. Thank you mum. I love you.

I suffer from Borderline Personality Disorder, or Emotional Intensity Disorder, whichever you prefer to use. They both mean the same thing. We're pretty much screwed up in the head, or at least that is the way this makes you feel, and how society makes you feel. But trust me your not. You are you, and you are unique just like everyone else.

There are approximately 5.9% of people in the United States suffer from this illness, if you can call it an illness. The word 'illness' gives you hope that you will be able to take pills and it will all disappear. I'm afraid to tell you that you are stuck with this for life. It will get easier to deal with over time, and as you get older you will find ways of coping with it. Some ways will be better than others, but in the end they all work.

I have suffered from this since I was about 9 or 10. I am now 23 and still living with this, and still finding ways of coping. I have been in and out of psychiatric units because like many who suffer from this, I have suicidal tendencies. This is something that we can't help, and as long as you have a good support network around you, this is something you will easily overcome. Not everyone will understand what you have, and some will stigmatise you because of it, but don't let them get to you. You are special.

When I was suffering quite badly, a nurse in one of the hospitals told me that people who hear voices are special, because we are the ones who have evolved to be able to hear our thoughts talking to us, whereas the others around us are still yet to evolve. This is something that made me feel a bit better about my voices, even though most of the things I hear are pretty nasty stuff. Now I know it is difficult hearing things that you know yourself aren't real, and that others can't hear, but if you focus on the fact that you know they aren't real and you know that it is not your fault, then this does sometimes help to put your mind at ease.

One of the other things that are associated with Borderline is the mood changes. Now these can be a real pain in the backside because they happen so suddenly and without any warning. They aren't just happy or sad mood changes either. Oh no, suffering from BPD we get the whole spectrum of moods. We can be happy one moment, and for no reason, be crying the next, and then all of a sudden as if someone has flicked a switch inside our head, we can become child-like and hyper. All of this can be exhausting for the person suffering from it, but one saving grace for us is that most BPD suffers seem to be amazingly good at hiding our emotions from those we don't want knowing. You have to know the sufferer well enough to be able to see behind the mask. This is like a protective barrier to us, because people can't judge us and badger us if they don't know how we are feeling. But on the same hand, this can make us feel lonely, as no one knows how we feel.

Most BPD sufferers get accused of making mountains out of molehills as the expression goes, but this is only because we are more sensitive to change, and more sensitive to the little things, so they have a greater effect on us. Our emotional threshold is already lower than everyone else's, and it also takes us a lot longer to come down from a bad turn, so we tend to boil over into meltdown quicker than your average Joe Bloggs. Unless people understand what is wrong with you, and you have the patience to help them if not, then people will judge you over this, and make you feel like a freak. But you are not a freak. Just keep in your head that you are unique, and you are you, and that is one thing that no one will ever be able to take away from you, no matter how hard they try to.

There are loads of different things that BPD sufferers have, and not every sufferer will have the self same signs as everyone else. I myself am a bad self harmer, whereas my partner's mother is not. Everyone is different, and deals with this in different ways. I used to rely heavily on alcohol to deal with the pain that I was feeling inside with this. I felt like no one understood how I felt, and I felt horribly alone. I was surrounded by people who loved me, but I never felt loved myself. This is common for people who suffer with this, but just remember this; no matter how alone you feel, or how low your life seems at that moment in time, there will always be someone there for you to pull you out of your never ending darkness and back into the light. Whether it be your family, a partner, a best friend, or even an animal, you are never alone.

Now as I said earlier I have been in hospital a fair few times with this, whether it was due to a suicide attempt, or because I had gotten myself blind drunk and passed out (quite literally), but from my experiences being in a hospital for a prolonged period of time with BPD is not a good idea. You begin to fear the world outside the hospital because you know you are safe in there. You can't harm yourself, and no one can harm you, your taken care of, and you are around people who can help. But hospital stays that are prolonged never end up helping, they hinder your recovery more than anything.

When I was a teen I spent six months in a psychiatric hospital for young adolescents, and by the end of the six months, I had managed to trick everyone in that place into believing I was all better and would never do anything to myself again. But worst of all, I feared going home. I feared having to return to the place where I had tried ending it all for the second time, I feared being alone with my brother, I feared seeing the people who had ruined my life and made me the way I am. But worst of all, I feared being left on my own. I had spent six months having my every move monitored because I was suicidal; I even had to be watched in the bath because I had tried to drown myself in the bath tub while I was in there. When you know that you have the security of being watched, you feel safe, and then having to give that all up completely and not be integrated back into family life is scary and it is a big change.

Change. Now that is one thing that BPD sufferers fear. Having structure, and knowing what is going to happen is safe, and safe is good. Safe is, well, safe. We know what is going to happen and when, and this means that we have no unexpected surprises that are going through us into blind panic. Some of can deal with change better than others. I've grown to get used to it over the years. I've had some big changes in my life so far that I've had to get used to, and although it is hard, it is something that is going to happen in life, and the sooner that you prepare yourself for it the better off you'll be. Now

I know myself that it is easier said than done, but it is possible. Trust me on that one.

Now then, before we go any further, one thing that I should probably discuss is eating disorders, because this is something that comes with this disorder. Now when you say eating disorders, what comes into your head? Anorexia? Bulimia? Skinny, unattractive sticks that call themselves fat? Yes, those are types of eating disorders, but what would you say if I said that binge eating was a type of eating disorder? Don't believe me? Google it, it is one. I couldn't believe this myself when I was told either. But it is, and it is more common than you think. People with this disorder will have some form of an eating disorder, and with me mine varies. I can go from binge eating and hoarding food, to not eating at all for about a week or two. My eating habits depend on my moods, and this is the same for a lot of BPD people. Most people don't like to admit that they have a problem, but admitting it is the first step to helping yourself, and if you can get your eating disorder into remission, then you have succeeded in making yourself feel a bit better.

Another problem that BPD sufferers have to contend with is addiction. And I'm not just talking about alcohol or drug addiction. No. You can be addicted to self harming, food, exercise, gambling, shopping, etc. Anything that makes you feel good, even for a split second, can become an addiction, something you crave and need to help you. The only problem is that with addiction it becomes something that we have to do, and if we don't it is like our world falls apart around us, and everything suddenly becomes dark and wrong. But addiction is hard to fight when you crave that one thing to help you ease the symptoms. I have addictions myself, and this is something I find hard to admit. I have an addiction to alcohol. I use alcohol to numb the voices in my head and to block out the visual hallucinations that I see on a daily basis. I know from experience how hard addictions are to fight, but it takes a strong willed person to fight them, and if you suffer from BPD and are still fighting, then you have the inner strength to fight this. You will need a good strong support circle around you to help, but there are loads of places out there that can help with addiction.

Another thing that I am addicted to is sexual intercourse, which is also another problem that most people with BPD suffer from. It is something that makes us all feel good, and that is because it releases things called endorphins into your blood stream which help you feel good, and its this that's makes sex an addiction to people who crave that boost of happiness. But it is not something that I would ever recommend using to make you feel good. Sex is to be enjoyed with someone you care about, not to be used to make you feel good, because that can lead you into bad situations, which I myself have gotten into.

Now some BPD suffers act on impulse, which to be honest can be great in some circumstances, but then in others it can get you into some very sticky and nasty situations. Everyone has impulses, its natural. But the problem is BPD sufferers don't tend to think things through before they act, so we go ahead and act first and then think later, by which time its too late. We need to change our mind set so that we think before we act like most other people, but this is something that gets learned over time, and through making mistakes. Some learn quicker than others, but if you are anything like me, you are going to take a hell of a long time to learn from your mistakes.

Living with Borderline is difficult; I'll give you that. You are going to get a lot of ups and downs through your life, and things will affect you worse than they would others, but my advice is get a pet. I have two dogs, Smudge and Scruff, and I wouldn't be here today if it wasn't for them. They are my rocks. My dogs give me undying love, and it doesn't matter what you do to them, they will always meet you at the door when you come home and be all excited. With Smudge, she and I have a special bond. She knows when there is something up, and she knows when I am going to have a funny turn, because she will come and sit next to me and look up at me, and she'll inform my parents by getting them to follow her to me. She's saved my life on a few occasions just by being there next to me when I've been about to attempt to take my life. I could never end my life because I could never lose my dogs. They are my best friends, and they have been with me for the last seven years, and if it wasn't for them I don't know where I'd be now.

Although I do have a good support network with my family and my partner, I've not always had that. When I was younger, before we found out what I had, I never used to talk to anyone about my problems. I was victimised as a child by a group of bullies that were led by three sisters. They made my life a living hell, and tried taking my life on two or three occasions. They even tried taking my brother's life because he wouldn't tell them where I was. I was terrified to go into school each day, and although I had tried to tell my parents what was happening, they just brushed me off and told me to get on with it and stop acting like a drama queen. I put myself through hell for years in school before my parents finally realised the full extent of what was going on in school. But the teachers used to call me crazy, and tell me that I was mentally insane, and so did the school children. I was threatened in school and almost died because I am a chronic asthmatic. BPD tends to come about because of abuse, and mine was physical, mental and emotional abuse at the hands of bullies.

What people don't seem to realise is that there are people out there who look and act like there is nothing wrong with them, but in actual fact they could be dying emotionally on the inside, and this is unfair to them, and to the people who they eventually snap at. There is so much stigma out there attached to mental health, and with BPD there is always other underlying mental health issues, whether its Obsessive Compulsive Disorder, Depression, Anxiety issues, anything like that. Having Borderline is bad enough, but having to deal with the stigma attached to it makes its harder, and it is this stigma that makes us feel like we are crazy, as if this is somehow our fault. Well let me tell you now, none of this is anyone's fault. If you have BPD then it will come out in you at some point in your life. But it can sometimes be genetic, sometimes its not. But there is nothing that can be done about this. Tablets don't help, as it's not chemical, it's emotional. And unfortunately there is no cure for this. Sometimes I just wish that I could snap my fingers and wake up, like this is all a dream, but then I look around me and realise that although yeah I have mental health problems, and yes I do struggle with day-to-day tasks, and I can't go into crowds and things, but all of this makes me who I am, and I'm thankful for that.

Having Borderline Personality Disorder may make you feel rubbish and worthless, but at least there are people out there who can help you deal with the way you are, and help you make sense of it all. I have resolved to help people, who suffer from this, and I use my experiences to help people, and this is how I cope with my disorder. I use it for the better, rather than letting it get me down again.

People will try and tell you that you can't do this, or that. But to them I say:

'I am strong. I have been through so much, and there is still so much I have yet to do. I am me. I am who I am, and there is nothing that anyone is going to do to change that. I have inner strength and I will use this to fight what I have'. Don't let anyone stand in the way of what you want to do with your life. Use your disorder to better yourself. See it as a challenge that you will have to battle daily, and for each day that you go through and survive, you are one day closer to conquering your disorder and getting your life back on track.